GW00382169

One In A Million

One In A Million

A book of poems where maths becomes fun

Chosen by Moira Andrew

Illustrated by
Sally Kindberg

VIKING

For David and Katherine

VIKING
Published by the Penguin Group
Penguin Books Ltd, 27 Wrights Lane, London W8 5TZ, England
Penguin Books USA Inc., 375 Hudson Street, New York, New York 10014, USA
Penguin Books Australia Ltd, Ringwood, Victoria, Australia
Penguin Books Canada Ltd, 10 Alcorn Avenue, Toronto, Ontario, Canada M4V 3B2
Penguin Books (NZ) Ltd, 182–190 Wairau Road, Auckland 10, New Zealand

Penguin Books Ltd, Registered Offices: Harmondsworth, Middlesex, England

First published 1992
10 9 8 7 6 5 4 3 2 1

This selection copyright © Moira Andrew, 1992
Illustrations copyright © Sally Kindberg, 1992

The moral right of the illustrator has been asserted

Filmset in Linotron 202 Times by
Rowland Phototypesetting Ltd, Bury St Edmunds, Suffolk

Printed in Great Britain by
Butler and Tanner Ltd, Frome and London

A CIP catalogue record for this book is available from the British Library

ISBN 0-670-84208-7

Contents

MONEY AND SHOPPING

SIZE AND COMPARISON

TIME, DAYS AND DATES

HEIGHT, WEIGHT AND MEASUREMENT

9

NUMBER AND
COUNTING

Because of Number One

I'll tell you something funny –
The strangest thing under the sun.
There's never an end to numbers,
Because of Number One.

You think you're clever when you count to
    twenty –
But then there's twenty-one.
So on you go, and thirty comes –
And then comes thirty-one!

You reach a hundred! Then you think
That all your counting's done.
But no! A little voice inside
Says, 'Now a hundred-and-one!'

You reach a thousand! Number One
Insists on going on.
You're all worn out. A million comes:
But there's still 'A million-and-one.'

The person who caused all this trouble
(When I could be out having fun)
Is the man who lived in the dim distant past
And invented Number One!

Pam Gidney

What is a Million?

The blades of grass growing
   on your back lawn.
The people you've met
   since the day you were born.

The age of a fossil
   you found by the sea.
The years it would take you
   to reach Octran Three.

The water drops needed
   to fill the fish pool.
The words you have read
   since you started school.

Wes Magee

In Daisy's Secret Drawer

ONE yellow ribbon,
TWO paper-clips,
THREE love letters,
FOUR hair-grips,
FIVE cassettes of pop songs,
SIX felt-tips,
SEVEN bits of chewed-up string,
EIGHT orange pips,
NINE plastic thingamybobs,
TEN bags of crisps.

Matt Simpson

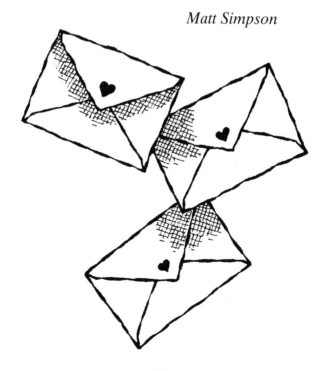

Family Visit

Two on a motor bike,
Four in a car,
Six people go to visit
Granny and Grandpa.

Eight people chattering,
In comes Uncle Jim
With cousins Luke and Kylie
And their little brother Tim.

There are so many of us
We can hardly shut the door:
Granny's only got ten chairs
So two sit on the floor.

I help Granny cut the cake,
Twelve slices for our tea.
Baby Tim won't eat and so
There's an extra piece for me.

Edna Eglinton

Muddy Mongrel

One paw
two paws
three paws
four
thousand
paw marks
on the
floor.

       Gina Douthwaite

Numbers

0   is the moon when it's round and full
1   is a blade of grass,
2   is a duck on a river or pool
3   a bird flying past.

4   is a yacht or a kiss with a tail
5   is an S gone flat,
6   is a snail with a silver trail
7   the ear of a cat.

8   is a snake in a twisted loop
9   a balloon on a string,
10 is a stick and a running hoop
    I roll round in a ring.

Catherine Benson

On My Way to School Today!

On my way to school today
I counted:
10 trees,
48 houses,
7 shops,
5 post-boxes,
15 people,
6 dogs,
3 cats,
51 cars,
4 lorries,
23 lamp-posts,
2 zebra crossings,
4 telephone kiosks,
and
1 park,
which I had just reached the end of,
when I realized it was SATURDAY!

Ian Souter

Ten Red Geraniums

Ten red geraniums
sprouting when it's fine,
a slug came slithering
and then there were nine.

Nine red geraniums
glowing when it's late,
a bat came blundering
and then there were eight.

Eight red geraniums
shining bright as heaven,
a magpie moth came munching
and then there were seven.

Seven red geraniums
propped up by sticks,
a wire-worm came wriggling
and then there were six.

Six red geraniums
fiery and alive,
a weevil came wandering
and then there were five.

Five red geraniums
dancing by the door,
a beetle came biting
and then there were four.

Four red geraniums
as vivid as can be,
a caterpillar came crawling
and then there were three.

Three red geraniums
petals all brand-new,
a ladybird came lunching
and then there were two.

Two red geraniums
blazing in the sun,
a great-aunt came admiring
and then there was one.

One red geranium –
the only one I've got,
I'll keep it on my window-sill
in its own well-watered pot.

Moira Andrew

21

Nature's Numbers

One old observant owl
Two tame tickled trout
Three thirsty throated thrushes
Four fine fantailed fish
Five fantastically famous frogs
Six swiftly swimming salmon
Seven sweetly singing songbirds
Eight engagingly eager eels
Nine nippy neighbourly newts
Ten tenderly tiptoeing tortoises.

John Cotton

How Many Peas . . .

How many peas
fit in a thimble?
How many acorns
fit in a matchbox?
How many ping-pong balls
fit in your shoe?
How many baked beans
fit in you?

Charles Thomson

Favouritism

When we caught measles
It wasn't fair –
My brother collected
Twice his share.

He counted my spots:
'One hundred and twenty!'
Which sounded to me
As if I had plenty.

Then I counted his –
And what do you think?
He'd two hundred and thirty-eight,
Small, round and pink!

I felt I'd been cheated
So 'Count mine again!'
I told him, and scowled
So he dared not complain.

'One hundred and twenty' –
The same as before . . .
In our house, he's youngest
And he always gets more!

Trevor Harvey

Adding it up

One tomato and one tomato
make two tomatoes.
Two bananas and two bananas
make four bananas.
Four jellies and four jellies
make eight jellies.
Eight feet and eight feet
make sixteen feet.
Sixteen feet in heavy boots
stamping on
eight jellies, four bananas and two tomatoes
make
a horrid mess.

Dave Calder

The Falling Star

When we lived in a city
(three flights up and down)
I never dreamed how many stars
could show above a town.

When we moved to a village
where lighted streets were few,
I thought I could see A L L the stars,
but, oh, I never knew –

Until we built a cabin
where hills are high and far,
I never knew how many
                    many
                        stars there really are!

Sara Teasdale

One, Two, Three

One star
to guide them,
three gifts to lay
on the dusty stable floor, for
One Child in the hay.

One ox
to low there,
two donkeys to bray;
three wise men to gaze upon
One Child in the hay.

Judith Nicholls

Numberless!

If all the numbers in the world were
rubbed out,
removed,
taken away:
I wouldn't know how old I was,
I wouldn't know the time of day,
I wouldn't know which bus to catch,
I wouldn't know the number of goals I had
    scored,
I wouldn't know how many scoops of ice-cream I
    had,
I wouldn't know my phone number,
I wouldn't know the page on my reading book,
I wouldn't know how tall I was,
I wouldn't know how much I weighed,
I wouldn't know how many sides there are in a
    hexagon,
I wouldn't know how many days in the month,
I wouldn't be able to work my calculator.
And I wouldn't be able to play hide-and-seek!
But I would know,
as far as my mum was concerned,
I was still her NUMBER ONE!

Ian Souter

SHAPE AND PATTERN

A Witch's Hat is not Like any Other Hat

A witch's hat is not
like any other hat.

It's not like
a school cap
a top hat
a silly hat
a nightcap
a beret
a Princess Di hat
a bowler hat
a woolly hat
a flat cap
a floppy hat
a hard hat
a bonnet
a helmet
a skull-cap.

It's not like
any of these hats

because it's
black
pointed
with stars
and a moon on

and it's mine.

Sue Stewart

31

Shapes

Dance in a circle hand in hand.
Draw a square with a stick in the sand.
Watch how three acrobats can dangle
From their trapeze in a triangle.
Then, when it's bedtime, jiggle
And giggle
And wiggle
And wriggle
Out of your tracksuit to make it fall
On the floor in a squiggle,
'Cause a squiggle's the nicest shape of all.

Leo Aylen

I'd Like to Squeeze

I'd like to squeeze this round world
into a new shape

I'd like to squeeze this round world
like a tube of toothpaste

I'd like to squeeze this round world
fair and square

I'd like to squeeze it and squeeze it
till everybody had an equal share

John Agard

hose

The hose
Can squeeze
Water to
A silver rod
That digs
Hard holes
In the mud,

Or, muzzled
Tighter by
The nozzle,
Can rain
Chill diamond
Chains
Across the yard,

Or, fanned
Out fine,
Can hang
A silk
Rainbow
Halo
Over soft fog.

Val Worth

Square

I F I W A S

S Q U A R E

W O U L D Y

O U C O M E

R O U N D T

O S E E M E

John Coldwell

Thoughts in a Launderette

My washing's going round and round I left that red sock in it's dyeing Matthew's shirt and Ian's football kit he'll kill me what will mum say about the pink pillowcases I'll say the lady put them in for me yes that's what I'll say . . .

Rita Ray

Balloon

as
big as
ball as round
as sun . . . I tug
and pull you when
you run and when
wind blows I
say polite
ly
H
O
L
D
M
E
T
I
G
H
T
L
Y.

Colleen Thibaudeau

Choosing Wallpaper

From floor to ceiling
My room could seem a garden,
With the same bright flower
Growing again and again.

The walls could be full as a shop
With toys and games,
Not just one of each
But rows and rows of the same.

Or in square after square
Could be a racing car,
Or a rocket travelling
In space to the stars.

Once the wallpaper's up
There it will have to stick;
It's hard, when I like them all,
To know which pattern to pick.

Stanley Cook

How a Good Greyhound is Shaped

A head like a snake,
a neck like a drake,
a back like a beam,
a belly like a bream,
a foot like a cat,
a tail like a rat.

Anonymous

Starfish and Other Shapes

If I had to choose a shape,
I think the one the starfish has is best,
with five arms, or more,
and a mouth at the centre of myself!

I could live in a tangle of seaweed,
or, like the reflection
of a fallen star,
be seen floating in rock pools.

As a globe-shaped sea-urchin,
with long, smooth spines,
I could live on the lower shore
under a cluster of stones.

If I choose to be leaf-shaped,
like the flat, sea worm, I could glide
through the waves. Or, as a round,
red, ribbon worm, I might burrow in sand.

If I kept on swimming, I might resemble
the pen-like shape of a common squid,
or take on the umbrella look
of a floating jellyfish!

I still think that to be shaped like a star
would be fun,
yet I cannot imagine being any shape
but the one I am!

Doris Corti

Shapes and Patterns

Have you seen the snowflakes falling?
    Have you watched them fly
from a grey and dappled distance
    in the far sky?

Each one has a different pattern
    sharp with points of light.
Soon, they'll make a quilted blanket –
    winter white.

Jean Kenward

The Sunflower

Round and round, round and round
I see the pattern go.
How many seeds are there?
And how can I reach to know?

The sunflower bends her heavy head,
I stand up on tiptoe.
My finger strokes her freckled face
As I follow the spiral's flow.

But oh! there are so many,
And my counting is so slow.

Catherine Benson

MONEY AND SHOPPING

Penny Poem

I had five little pennies
going to the shop
enough for some sweets
but none for pop

One sweet for Mum
one sweet for Dad
and one sweet for my brother
who isn't so bad

One sweet for tea-time
leaves one sweet for me
should I eat it right now
or . . . Hmm, delicious!

John Walsh

Treats

My great-uncle George came.
He gave me a £.
I went to the toy shop
And looked all around.

I bought John some marbles
And a paint-box for me.
The man took my £
And said, 'Here's 40p.

The paint-box was 50,
The marbles were 10.
You've still got some left
So please call again.'

I went to the baker's
For 2 currant buns.
He took all my money
And gave me 10 1s.

I stopped at the sweet-shop
For 10 penny sweets.
Now all my £'s gone –
But I've got lots of treats!

Pam Gidney

Shopping Basket

I bought two loaves of bread.
I bought one joint of meat.
I bought three big green apples.
I bought one sticky sweet.
I bought one custard-pie.
How many things did I buy?

Charles Thomson

See a Penny

See a penny
Pick it up –
All the day you'll have good luck.

One hundred pennies
Make a pound,
One hundred days –
Keep your eyes on the ground!

Three months,
One week,
And a day or two –
Then you'll find your lucky pound
Saved up for you.

Dave Ward

Two Lists

I'm going out now
To the shops for my dad

I've got two lists
One of things to buy

Carrots
Peas
Bread
An apple-pie

One of things to remember:

> *Don't talk to strangers*
> *Go straight there*
> *Be careful crossing the roads*
> *Don't talk to strangers*
> *Come straight back*
> *Don't lose the money*
> *Don't talk to strangers*
> *Don't get lost*
> *Don't forget the change*

And Tommy . . .

Yes, Dad?

Don't talk to strangers

I'm back now from going
To the shops for my dad

I didn't talk to strangers
I went straight there
I was careful crossing the roads
I didn't talk to strangers
I came straight back
I didn't lose the money
I didn't talk to strangers
I didn't get lost
I didn't forget the change
And . . . I didn't talk to strangers

So what did you forget?
Dad said

The carrots
The peas
The apple-pie
And . . .

Yes?

The bread

Tony Bradman

Uncle David

Uncle David was very tall
and very rich. To us children
he was like a lamp-post, bent
at the neck and almost always
stooped to avoid low
lintels. And rich? Well, we
thought he was – he kept a
stock of half-crowns in a
steel safe in the hall.

Saturdays were a ritual.
Uncle David would stand us
in front of him, bend down
to inquire of our behaviour
during the week. We thought
he could see right into the
back of our brains. Satisfied,
he'd dig deep into his pocket,
produce dungeon-black keys.

Hushed, we waited. He'd
punch in magic numbers, open
the massive door. He'd take
another smaller key, fit it
into a metal drawer, reach in
for a drawstring bag
heavy with silver half-crowns.
One for each of us. Our parents
smiled behind their hands.

They knew, you see, that
Uncle David was known in
the family as a Scrooge,
gloating over his fat bank
balance, his store of coins,
his sleek-nosed car.
We craned our necks to look
up at him. To us he was just
very tall – and very rich.

Moira Andrew

Fifty Pence

'Lend us fifty pence, please, Granpa.'
'Fifty pence. What would you be wanting with
    fifty pence?'
'To buy some sweets.'
'In my day, I used to work a week to earn fifty
    pence.
Or ten shillings as it was in proper money.
I'd come home on Friday night,
Give it all to my mum,
I didn't even open the envelope.
Then she'd hand me sixpence.'

'What you could do with sixpence.
You could go to football on Saturday afternoon,
Drink yourself roaring in the evening
Take your girl to the pictures. Every night.
And buy her a box of chocolates,
And a bunch of flowers,
And go out for a fish supper.
And do you know what?
I still managed to save a pound a week.'

'Here, Granpa,
Could you lend us one of those sixpences instead.'

John Coldwell

SIZE AND COMPARISON

magnifying glass

Small grains
In a stone
Grow edges
That twinkle;

The smooth
Moth's wing
Sprouts feathers
Like shingles;

My thumb
Is wrapped
In rich
Satin wrinkles.

Val Worth

The Biggest

I'm not as big
and fat as Pat
or as slim and
small as Paul.

Scrooge is huge
but a digger is bigger,
so Paul is the smallest,
the digger's the biggest

(and best
for moving the earth!).

Peter Comaish

The Kitten

The trouble with a kitten is
THAT
Eventually it becomes a
CAT.

Ogden Nash

from Crafty Creatures

The flea is small
And no one's pet
But likes to hear
Of Dogs to Let.

Max Fatchen

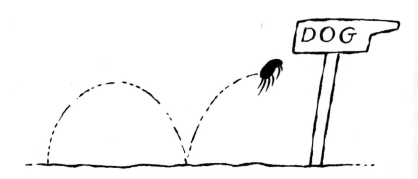

I Want a Small Piece of String

I want a small piece of string with an ant on it carrying a small piece of string with a worm on it carrying a small piece of string with a cat on it carrying a small piece of string with a dog on it carrying a small piece of string with a cow on it carrying a small piece of string with a horse on it carrying a small piece of string with a bird on it carrying a small piece of string with a rhinoceros on it carrying a small piece of string with a dinosaur on it carrying a small piece of string with a small piece of string with a small piece of string with an elephant on it carrying a small piece of string with a small piece of string on it.

Remy Charlip

Giant's Wife

The terrible giant had a wife
   Who was almost twelve feet tall.
She slept with her head in the kitchen
   And her feet way out in the hall.

Anonymous

When the Giant Stays for Breakfast

When the giant stays for breakfast
He eats his Cornflakes with a spade,
Followed by a lorry-load
Of toast and marmalade.
Next, he takes a dustbin
That's filled with tea,
Drinks it all in one gulp,
And leaves the washing-up to me.

John Coldwell

The Fly

How large unto the tiny fly
Must little things appear! –
A rosebud like a feather bed,
Its prickle like a spear;

A dewdrop like a looking-glass,
A hair like golden wire;
The smallest grain of mustard seed
As fierce as coals of fire;

A loaf of bread, a lofty hill;
A wasp, a cruel leopard;
And specks of salt as bright to see
As lambkins to a shepherd.

Walter de la Mare

Who Can Tell?

How big is a dinosaur egg?
Bigger than a tennis ball,
smaller than a tree?
Taller than a turtle shell
but not as tall as me?
Who can see?

How hard is a dinosaur egg?
Harder than a chicken's
but not as hard as steel?
Tough enough to make you think
it isn't really real?
Who can feel?

What might hatch from a dinosaur egg?
Diplodocus, stegosaurus
with its spiny tail?
Allosaurus, brontosaurus
tapping at the shell?
Who can tell?

Judith Nicholls

The Conjuror

He magicked a spider,
He magicked a bat,
He magicked two doves
That flew out of his hat.

I said, 'But that's small stuff!'
He tried once again,
But all that he magicked
Was a bantam hen.

I looked down my nose.
'Do you call that *big*?' –
He puffed and he strained
And he magicked a pig.

'That's more like it!' I said,
'But I've seen an old witch
Magic whales as big
As a football pitch!'

'*You* couldn't magic a
Small tiger,' I bet him.
But he *did*. – And to prove it
The tiger ATE HIM!

Raymond Wilson

Sorting

I wouldn't call
   an insect TALL . . .
I wouldn't call it
   SHORT.
I'd call it tiny
   if I had
to send in
   a report.

But everything
   is relative.
An ogre,
   I suppose,
might think
   a hippopotamus
as dainty
   as a rose!

So which is which
   and what is what
in every kind
   of being
is very hard
   to certify.
It's all a way
   of seeing.

Jean Kenward

all kinds of trees

on the park
there are trees
with leaves
shaped like hands

others have
silvery bark

some trees grow tall
some trees stay small
and some grow so broad
and so high and so grand
they must see things
that happen
all over the land
round about.

Joan Poulson

The Moon in a Balloon

Puff, puff.

Puff, puff
   and the balloon grows.
How big?
  Big enough to hold . . .
     shoelaces this long.

Puff, puff (cheeks blushing)
   and the red balloon grows.
How big?
  Big enough to hold . . .
     shoelaces this long
     and their pair of shoes this large.

Puff, puff (cheeks glowing)
   and the bright red balloon grows.
How big?
  Big enough to hold . . .
     shoelaces this long
     and their pair of shoes this large,
     worn by a girl this tall.

Puff, puff (cheeks flaming)
   and the big bright red balloon grows.
How big?
  Big enough to hold . . .
     shoelaces this long
     and their pair of shoes this large,
     worn by a girl this tall,
     next to a boy this wide.

Puff, puff (cheeks roaring)
        and the very big bright red balloon
grows.
How big?
    Big enough to hold . . .
        shoelaces this long
        and their pair of shoes this large,
        worn by a girl this tall,
        next to a boy this wide,
        with a little dog (woof woof).

Puff, puff (cheeks raging)
        and the very, very big bright red balloon
grows.
How big?
    Big enough to hold . . .
        shoelaces this long
        and their pair of shoes this large,
        worn by a girl this tall,
        next to a boy this wide,
        with a little dog (woof woof).
        They're all standing on the moon!

What a very, very, very big bright red balloon.

No more puff, puff,
blowing up such big balloons is much too tough.

Your turn, here you are.

Oh no,
don't let it go o   o   o   o   o   o

o

o

o

o   o

o   o

o

o   o

o   o

o

o   o

o

o   o   o

o

o

o   o

o   o

o

o

o

Mike Johnson

Smaller than a Giant

Goliath the Philistine
Was a giant of a man
And how tall was he?
Six cubits and a span.

Six times the length of a forearm
And once from little finger to thumb:
No wonder his enemies trembled
When they saw Goliath come.

Why not measure yourself
With your arm and your hand
And find how much smaller
You would stand?

Stanley Cook

I'm Big

I'm big
I'm very big
Because I'm very big
I can grab your pen
and you're scared
to try and get your pen back
because I'm big.
Very big.

> *But* I've heard that
> when people grow up
> some people grow faster
> than others.

> This means that
> when I'm grown up
> you may be big
> and I may be
> not so big.

This is one of the things I worry about.

Michael Rosen

Gwyneth's Book of Records

I wonder what it's like to be
the fattest person in the world?

Is it better to be tallest or the smallest,
or best to be the person
who's exactly in the middlest?

The loudest and the quietest shouldn't live next
   door,
but the strongest and the weakest
could even share a house,
go in and out together, laugh and cry
and be in love;
could the slowest and the fastest?

The thinnest person might be Dad or Mum,
or daughter, brother, sister, son
of the bravest, handsomest
or ugliest . . .

When I grow up I want to be the happiest person
in the world

and I don't care if only I know I am.

Mike Johnson

Friendly Warning

LISTEN GRASS, TAKE
IT EASY. DON'T GROW
TOO TALL. THEY'LL JUST
BRING IN A LAWN
MOWER AND CUT
YOU DOWN SHORT.

SEE? I TOLD YOU THEY WOULD.

Robert Froman

SMALL, smaller

I thought I knew all there was to know
Of being small, until I saw once, black against the
   snow,
A shrew, trapped in my footprint, jump and fall
And jump again and fall, the hole too deep, the
walls
   too tall.

Russell Hoban

TIME, DAYS AND DATES

Days

What are days for?
Days are where we live.
They come, they wake us
Time and time over.
They are to be happy in:
Where can we live but days?

Ah, solving that question
Brings the priest and the doctor
In their long coats
Running over the fields.

Philip Larkin

Socks

On Monday we wear quiet socks
Not flash, bang start a riot socks,
Not, Hey you come and try it socks.
On Monday we wear quiet socks.

On Tuesday we wear plain socks,
Not crazy and insane socks,
Not frazzle up your brain socks.
On Tuesday we wear plain socks.

On Wednesday we wear boring socks,
Not pass to me goal-scoring socks,
Not modern abstract drawing socks.
On Wednesday we wear boring socks.

On Thursday. Ordinary socks,
Not horror, shock and scary socks,
Not beastly monsters hairy socks.
On Thursday. Ordinary socks.

On Friday, it's polite socks,
Not glowing in the night socks,
Not give your aunt a fright socks.
On Friday it's polite socks.

At weekends we wear loud socks,
That stand out in the crowd socks
And make our feet feel proud socks.
At weekends we wear loud socks.

John Coldwell

I Wasn't Expecting Thursday

I woke up.
There, at the end of my bed,
Looking as mean as
A broken shoelace,
A missed bus,
A forgotten lunch-box
And a cut knee,
Was,

THURSDAY

It folded its great hairy arms
And barred the way.
'If you ever want to see
Friday again,' it growled,
'You'll have to get past me first.'
That's Thursday for you.

John Coldwell

First and Last

I'm the last one at school in the morning
and first out the door at night,
I'm the first one in the dinner queue
but the last to get my maths right.

I'm the last to help tidy up
and the first to switch on TV,
I'm the last to get out of bed
and the first home from school for my tea.

I'm the last to jump in the water
when we stand at the edge of the pool,
I'm the first to the ice-cream van
when it waits outside of my school.

I'm the last to finish my homework
and the first to the shop for sweets,
I'm the last to volunteer
but the first in line for treats!

Brian Moses

The Clock

Tick tack tock
goes the Grandpa clock.
It moves with every
minute.
It's got a great brass
pendulum
that's always swinging
in it.

And when the hour
comes round at last
it sings a special
song
and uses all
the strength it has:
BONG!

   BONG!

    BONG!

Jean Kenward

Timeless

There is no clock in the forest
but a dandelion to blow,
an owl that hunts
when the light has gone,
a mouse that sleeps till night has come,
lost in the moss below.

There is no clock in the forest,
only the cuckoo's song
and the thin white
of the early dawn,
the pale damp-bright
of a waking June,
the bluebell-light
of a day half-born
when the stars have gone.

There is no clock in the forest.

Judith Nicholls

A Hibernating Hedgehog

A hibernating hedgehog,
Woke up to greet the spring,
He'd set the alarm for half-past May,
But he hadn't heard it ring.
In fact he'd gone and overslept,
A silly thing to do,
Not only had he missed the spring,
He'd missed the summer too.

Martin Honeysett

The Work of Each Day

Wash on Monday,
Iron on Tuesday,
Mend on Wednesday,
Churn on Thursday,
Clean on Friday,
Bake on Saturday,
Rest on Sunday.

Traditional

Four Dates

William the Conqueror, ten sixty-six,
Played on the Saxons many cruel tricks.

Columbus sailed the ocean blue,
In fourteen hundred and ninety-two.

The Spanish Armada met its fate,
In fifteen hundred and eighty-eight.

In sixteen hundred and sixty-six,
London burnt like rotten sticks.

Traditional

Growing Old

When I was younger, I got away with a lot more
than I do now, Mother would fuss over me
if I said I didn't want to go to school,
or I had an upset tummy, now, it's get yourself
ready
and get off to school this minute,
my brother, Simon, he's three, he's the one
who gets all the special attention now,
I suppose as I'm seven I'm grown-up, so
it's only fair, besides,
his turn will come . . .

Bill Boyle

Between Birthdays

My birthdays take so long to start.
They come along a year apart.
It's worse than waiting for a bus;
I fear I used to fret and fuss,
But now, when by impatience vexed
Between one birthday and the next,
I think of all that I have seen
That keeps on happening in between.
The songs I've heard, the things I've done,
Make my un-birthdays not so un-

Ogden Nash

HEIGHT, WEIGHT AND MEASUREMENT

Chat

The See-saw

Tom sitting all alone
At the end of the see-saw
Lowers it by his weight
With a bump to the floor.

But on to the other end
Climbs Harry, his brother,
And they're the same weight
And balance each other.

And Harry's joined
By their sister and the cat
And down goes their end
For Tom's not as heavy as that.

Stanley Cook

Which?

Would you rather be
Thin
as
a
Pin
or
Lean
as
a
Sardine?
Or do you agree
It would be better if you were as Thick as an old oak tree
Fat as a pig, or harvest pumpkin, or dusty honey bee?

O dear me, no,
I don't want to become
Tiny like Tom Thumb
or grow
Small enough to live with a mouse
in his house;

I don't want to be as Big as an elephant, Wider than a bus,
Huge as a fairy tale giant or a hippopotamus,
I think I'd rather stay
Just as I am if I may,
The same size tomorrow as yesterday.

Leonard Clark

94

Short Story

I
wrote
a
great
story
at
school
today
Mum
It
was
60
c
e
n
t
i
m
e
t
r
e
s
l o n g

David R. Morgan

Skip-rope Song

One
two,
skip over my shoe.

Three
four,
skip up to the door.

Five
six
skip over the sticks.

Seven
eight . . .
wait, wait.
Don't skip
too high,
too far,
too fast,
or who
knows where
you'll land
at last?
There was
a girl
lived in
our town
who skipped
so high

she
 never
  came
   down.

I. O. Eastwick

Down to Earth

I climbed a tree,
I got too high,
My dad said I could
Touch the sky.

But I fell down,
And bumped my head.
So I think I'll stick
To the ground instead.

Tony Bradman

My Friend Dee

My friend Dee
Is bigger than me,
And I'm more than three feet tall.
My friend Dee
Is bigger than me –
She can see over next-door's wall.

Whenever she looks over,
She laughs and giggles
Or runs and hides
And screams and shivers,
But she *never* tells me
What it is she can see . . .
Of course *I'm* not bothered at all.

Dave Ward

my granny has a lot of chairs

in granny's house
there are chairs
everywhere

and some are high
and some are low
some are round
some are square

some chairs are patterned
others are plain
but the one I like to
sit on again and again
belonged to granny
when she was small

and it's the squashy-fat,
red-painted one, her
little rocking chair.

Joan Poulson

The How-Tall? Wall

Every birthday and New Year's Day,
Mum stands us up against the kitchen wall,
And Dad takes his flat carpenter's pencil
And marks our height with a neat line,
   A neat line, firm and straight,
    And writes our names and the date.

My lines have climbed slowly up the wall,
As each birthday came along,
Getting higher and higher and higher
But not as high as Tracy's, although
   They are further up than Tracy's used to be
   When I was one and she was three.

My marks are way above Keith's
But even his have gone up a bit.
Still, I'll always be older than him
And I'll always be younger than Trace.
   But will she always be the tallest.
   With me in the middle and Keith the smallest?

I asked Mum but she didn't know
I asked Dad and he told me
He used to be taller than Uncle Martin,
But I don't think that can really be true.
   My Uncle Martin is six foot four
   He has to stoop down to come in the door.

Gerard Benson

101

Give up Slimming, Mum

My Mum
is short
and plump
and pretty
and I wish
she'd give up
slimming.

So does Dad.

Her cooking's
delicious –
you can't
beat it –
but you really can
hardly bear
to eat it –
the way she sits
with her eyes
brimming,
watching you
polish off
the spuds
and trimmings
while she
has nothing
herself but a small
thin dry
diet biscuit:
that's all.

My Mum
is short
and plump
and pretty
and I wish
she'd give up
slimming.

So does Dad.

She says she
looks as though
someone had
sat on her –
BUT WE LIKE MUM
WITH A BIT
OF FAT ON HER!

Kit Wright

The Fat Lady's Request

I, too, will disappear, will
Escape into centuries of darkness.

Come here and give me a cuddle,
Sit on my lap and give me a hug

While we are both still enjoying
This mysterious whirling planet.

And if you find me fat, you find me
Also, easy to find, very easy to find.

Joyce la Verne

Said a Long Crocodile

Said a very l–o–n–g crocodile,
'My length is a terrible trial!
   I know I should diet
   But each time I try it
I'm hungry for more than a mile!'

Lilian Moore

Ant

and Eleph-Ant

Said a tiny Ant
To the Elephant,
'Mind how you tread in this clearing!'

But alas! Cruel fate!
She was crushed by the weight
Of an Elephant, hard of hearing.

Spike Milligan

Every Child's Answer to that Telephone Query from a Distant Relative . . .

'Are you growing up fast?'
        'Yes, I've just hit the ceiling,
        Now I've gone through the roof
        And at present I'm kneeling
        To hear what you're saying,
        With my legs through the door,
        One arm through the window,
        My chin on the floor
        And my feet in the roadway,
        Which are causing a worry
        With a traffic jam stretching
        For ten miles through Surrey.

        So I'd better ring off . . .

        Bye.'

Trevor Harvey

Index of First Lines

Acknowledgements

By kind permission of John Agard c/o Caroline Sheldon Literary Agency 'I'd like to squeeze' reprinted from *You'll Love This Stuff* (Cambridge University Press, 1986); 'Shapes' by Leo Aylen, copyright © Leo Aylen, 1991 by permission of the author; 'Numbers' and 'The Sunflower' by Catherine Benson, copyright © Catherine Benson, 1991 by permission of the author; 'The How-Tall? Wall' by Gerard Benson, copyright © Gerard Benson, 1991 by permission of the author; 'Growing Old' by Bill Boyle, copyright © Bill Boyle, 1991; 'Down to Earth' and 'Two Lists' by Tony Bradman from *Smile Please!* by Tony Bradman (Viking Kestrel, 1987) copyright © Tony Bradman, 1987; 'Adding it up' by Dave Calder, copyright © Dave Calder, 1990 by permission of the author; 'Which?' by Leonard Clark reprinted from *Good Company* (Dobson, 1968) copyright © The Literary Executor of Leonard Clark by permission of The Literary Executor of Leonard Clark; 'Fifty Pence' by John Coldwell reprinted from *More Lasting Than a Fish Supper* (Salford Pocketbooks, 1988) copyright © John Coldwell, 1988, 'I wasn't expecting Thursday' by John Coldwell reprinted from *The Slack-Jawed Camel* (Stride, 1992) copyright © John Coldwell, 1992, 'Socks' by John Coldwell reprinted from *The Bees Knees* (Stride, 1990) copyright © John Coldwell, 1990, 'Square' by John Coldwell reprinted from *Daleks on Ramsay Street* (Salford Pocketbooks, 1988) copyright © John Coldwell, 1988, 'When a giant stays for breakfast' by John Coldwell, copyright © John Coldwell, 1990, all by permission of the author; 'The Biggest' by Peter Comaish, copyright © Peter Comaish, 1992 by permission of the author; 'Choosing Wallpaper', 'The See-Saw' and 'Smaller than a Giant' by Stanley Cook, copyright © Stanley Cook, 1991 by permission of the Literary Estate of Stanley Cook; 'Starfish and Other Shapes' by Doris Corti, copyright © Doris Corti, 1990 by permission of the author; 'Nature's Numbers' first published in *The Poetry File* by John Cotton, published by Macmillan Education/Nelson, 1989, by permission of the author; 'The Fly' by Walter de la Mare, by permission of the Literary Trustees of Walter de la Mare and the Society of Authors as their representative; 'Muddy Mongrel' by Gina Douthwaite, copyright © Gina Douthwaite, 1992 by permission of the author; 'Family Visit' by Edna Eglinton, copyright © Edna Eglinton, 1992, by permission of the author; 'Crafty Creatures' by Max Fatchen reprinted from *Wry Rhymes for Troublesome Times* (Viking Kestrel, 1983) copyright © Max Fatchen, 1983; 'Friendly Warning' by Robert Froman reprinted from *Seeing Things* (Thomas Crowell, 1944) copyright © Robert Froman, 1974, by permission of the author; 'Because of Number One' and 'Treats' by Pam Gidney, copyright © Pam Gidney, 1992 by permission of the author; 'Every Child's Answer to that Telephone Query from a Distant Relative' by Trevor Harvey reprinted from *Read a Poem, Write a Poem* (Basil Blackwell, 1991) copyright © Trevor Harvey, 1991 and 'Favouritism' by Trevor Harvey reprinted from *Poetry for Projects* (Scholastic, 1989) copyright © Trevor Harvey, 1989 by permission of the author; 'SMALL, smaller' by Russell Hoban reprinted from *The Pedalling Man* (Heinemann), copyright © Russell Hoban, by permission of David Higham Associates Limited; 'Hibernating Hedgehog' by Martin Honeysett reprinted from *Animal Nonsense Rhymes* (Methuen Children's Books, 1984), copyright © Martin Honeysett,